50 Traditional Japanese Meals for Home

By: Kelly Johnson

Table of Contents

- Sushi
- Sashimi
- Tempura
- Tonkatsu
- Okonomiyaki
- Takoyaki
- Yakitori
- Teriyaki Chicken
- Unagi Don
- Gyudon
- Katsudon
- Oyakodon
- Ten Don
- Chirashi Don
- Onigiri
- Miso Soup
- Chawanmushi
- Nikujaga
- Sukiyaki
- Shabu-Shabu
- Nabe
- Yosenabe
- Oden
- Hiyayakko
- Gyoza
- Karaage
- Agedashi Tofu
- Tamagoyaki
- Zaru Soba
- Kitsune Udon
- Nabeyaki Udon
- Somen
- Hiyashi Chuka
- Ochazuke
- Saba Shioyaki

- Tai Meshi
- Buta no Shogayaki
- Katsu Curry
- Hayashi Rice
- Omurice
- Hambagu
- Japanese Potato Salad
- Kinpira Gobo
- Tsukemono
- Daifuku
- Dorayaki
- Matcha Warabi Mochi
- Mitarashi Dango
- Anmitsu
- Taiyaki

Sushi (Japanese Vinegared Rice with Fillings)

Ingredients:

- 2 cups sushi rice
- 2 ½ cups water
- ¼ cup rice vinegar
- 1 tbsp sugar
- ½ tsp salt
- Nori sheets (for rolls)
- Fillings: raw fish, cucumber, avocado, cooked shrimp, or imitation crab

Instructions:

1. **Prepare Rice:** Rinse sushi rice, cook with water, then mix with vinegar, sugar, and salt. Let cool.
2. **Assemble Rolls (Maki):** Place nori on a bamboo mat, spread rice, add fillings, and roll tightly. Slice into pieces.
3. **Serve:** Enjoy with soy sauce, wasabi, and pickled ginger.

Sashimi (Thinly Sliced Raw Fish)

Ingredients:

- ½ lb sushi-grade fish (salmon, tuna, yellowtail)
- Soy sauce
- Wasabi
- Pickled ginger

Instructions:

1. **Slice Fish:** Use a sharp knife to cut fish into thin slices.
2. **Serve:** Arrange neatly and serve with soy sauce, wasabi, and ginger.

Tempura (Lightly Battered and Fried Seafood & Vegetables)

Ingredients:

- ½ cup all-purpose flour
- ½ cup ice-cold water
- 1 egg
- ½ lb shrimp, peeled and deveined
- 1 cup mixed vegetables (sweet potato, zucchini, bell pepper)
- Vegetable oil for frying

Instructions:

1. **Make Batter:** Whisk egg and ice water, then gently mix in flour (do not overmix).
2. **Coat & Fry:** Dip shrimp and vegetables in batter and fry in hot oil until golden.
3. **Serve:** Drain and serve with tempura dipping sauce.

Tonkatsu (Japanese Breaded Pork Cutlet)

Ingredients:

- 2 pork loin cutlets
- Salt and pepper to taste
- ½ cup flour
- 1 egg, beaten
- 1 cup panko breadcrumbs
- Oil for frying
- Tonkatsu sauce (store-bought or homemade)

Instructions:

1. **Coat Pork:** Season cutlets, dredge in flour, dip in egg, then coat with panko.
2. **Fry:** Deep-fry in hot oil until golden and crispy.
3. **Serve:** Slice and drizzle with tonkatsu sauce.

Okonomiyaki (Japanese Savory Pancake)

Ingredients:

- 1 cup flour
- ½ cup dashi or water
- 1 egg
- 1 cup shredded cabbage
- 2 tbsp green onions, chopped
- 2 tbsp tempura flakes (optional)
- 4 slices bacon
- Okonomiyaki sauce
- Mayonnaise
- Bonito flakes (katsuobushi)

Instructions:

1. **Make Batter:** Mix flour, dashi, and egg, then fold in cabbage and green onions.
2. **Cook Pancake:** Pour batter onto a hot griddle, top with bacon, and cook until golden.
3. **Serve:** Drizzle with okonomiyaki sauce, mayo, and bonito flakes.

Takoyaki (Octopus-Filled Dough Balls)

Ingredients:

- 1 cup flour
- 1 cup dashi or water
- 1 egg
- ½ cup chopped octopus
- 2 tbsp green onions
- 2 tbsp tempura flakes
- Takoyaki sauce
- Mayonnaise
- Bonito flakes

Instructions:

1. **Make Batter:** Whisk flour, dashi, and egg.
2. **Cook Takoyaki:** Heat a takoyaki pan, pour batter into the molds, and add octopus. Turn with skewers until golden.
3. **Serve:** Drizzle with takoyaki sauce, mayo, and bonito flakes.

Yakitori (Grilled Chicken Skewers)

Ingredients:

- 1 lb chicken thighs, cut into bite-sized pieces
- ½ cup soy sauce
- ¼ cup mirin
- 2 tbsp sugar
- 1 tsp grated ginger
- Bamboo skewers

Instructions:

1. **Marinate Chicken:** Mix soy sauce, mirin, sugar, and ginger, then marinate chicken for 30 minutes.
2. **Grill:** Thread onto skewers and grill over high heat, basting with marinade.
3. **Serve:** Enjoy with rice or as a snack.

Teriyaki Chicken

Ingredients:

- 2 boneless chicken thighs
- ¼ cup soy sauce
- 2 tbsp mirin
- 1 tbsp sugar
- 1 tsp grated garlic
- 1 tsp grated ginger

Instructions:

1. **Cook Chicken:** Sear chicken in a pan until golden.
2. **Add Sauce:** Mix soy sauce, mirin, sugar, garlic, and ginger. Pour over chicken and cook until thickened.
3. **Serve:** Slice and serve with rice.

Unagi Don (Grilled Eel Rice Bowl)

Ingredients:

- 1 fillet unagi (grilled eel, store-bought or fresh)
- 1 cup cooked rice
- 2 tbsp soy sauce
- 1 tbsp mirin
- 1 tbsp sugar

Instructions:

1. **Make Sauce:** Simmer soy sauce, mirin, and sugar until slightly thickened.
2. **Grill Eel:** Brush eel with sauce and grill until caramelized.
3. **Serve:** Place eel over rice and drizzle with more sauce.

Gyudon (Japanese Beef Bowl)

Ingredients:

- ½ lb thinly sliced beef (ribeye or sirloin)
- 1 onion, thinly sliced
- 1 cup dashi or beef broth
- 2 tbsp soy sauce
- 1 tbsp mirin
- 1 tbsp sugar
- 1 tsp grated ginger
- 1 cup cooked rice

Instructions:

1. **Sauté Onions:** Cook onions in dashi, soy sauce, mirin, sugar, and ginger until soft.
2. **Add Beef:** Add sliced beef and cook until just done.
3. **Serve:** Spoon beef mixture over rice and enjoy.

Katsudon (Pork Cutlet Rice Bowl)

Ingredients:

- 1 pork cutlet (tonkatsu), sliced
- 1 cup cooked rice
- ½ onion, sliced
- ½ cup dashi or chicken broth
- 2 tbsp soy sauce
- 1 tbsp mirin
- 1 tsp sugar
- 1 egg, beaten
- Green onions, chopped (for garnish)

Instructions:

1. **Simmer Onions & Sauce:** In a pan, cook onions in dashi, soy sauce, mirin, and sugar.
2. **Add Cutlet & Egg:** Place tonkatsu over onions, pour beaten egg on top, and cover until set.
3. **Serve:** Place over a bowl of rice and garnish with green onions.

Oyakodon (Chicken and Egg Rice Bowl)

Ingredients:

- 1 boneless chicken thigh, diced
- ½ onion, sliced
- ½ cup dashi
- 2 tbsp soy sauce
- 1 tbsp mirin
- 1 tsp sugar
- 1 egg, beaten
- 1 cup cooked rice
- Green onions (for garnish)

Instructions:

1. **Cook Chicken & Onions:** Simmer in dashi, soy sauce, mirin, and sugar.
2. **Add Egg:** Pour beaten egg over and cover until set.
3. **Serve:** Spoon over rice and garnish with green onions.

Ten Don (Tempura Rice Bowl)

Ingredients:

- ½ cup flour
- ½ cup ice-cold water
- 1 egg
- ½ lb shrimp and mixed vegetables (zucchini, sweet potato)
- Vegetable oil for frying
- 2 tbsp soy sauce
- 1 tbsp mirin
- 1 tsp sugar
- 1 cup cooked rice

Instructions:

1. **Make Tempura:** Mix batter, coat shrimp and vegetables, and fry until golden.
2. **Make Sauce:** Heat soy sauce, mirin, and sugar.
3. **Serve:** Place tempura over rice and drizzle with sauce.

Chirashi Don (Scattered Sushi Bowl)

Ingredients:

- 1 cup sushi rice
- ½ cup assorted sashimi (salmon, tuna, shrimp)
- ½ cucumber, thinly sliced
- 1 tbsp rice vinegar
- 1 tsp sugar
- ½ tsp salt
- 1 tbsp pickled ginger
- Wasabi & soy sauce for serving

Instructions:

1. **Prepare Rice:** Mix cooked rice with vinegar, sugar, and salt.
2. **Assemble Bowl:** Spread rice in a bowl, top with sashimi, cucumber, and ginger.
3. **Serve:** Enjoy with wasabi and soy sauce.

Onigiri (Japanese Rice Balls)

Ingredients:

- 2 cups cooked rice
- 1 tbsp salt
- 1 sheet nori, cut into strips
- Fillings (salmon, tuna mayo, pickled plum)

Instructions:

1. **Shape Rice Balls:** Wet hands with saltwater, form rice into triangles, and insert filling.
2. **Wrap in Nori:** Add a strip of nori for handling.
3. **Serve:** Enjoy as a snack or packed lunch.

Miso Soup

Ingredients:

- 3 cups dashi
- 2 tbsp miso paste
- ½ cup tofu, diced
- 1 tbsp wakame seaweed
- 1 green onion, sliced

Instructions:

1. **Heat Dashi:** Bring dashi to a simmer.
2. **Dissolve Miso:** Stir miso paste in a ladle with some dashi, then mix into the pot.
3. **Add Tofu & Wakame:** Simmer for a few minutes, then serve with green onions.

Chawanmushi (Japanese Savory Egg Custard)

Ingredients:

- 2 eggs
- 1 cup dashi
- ½ tsp soy sauce
- ½ tsp mirin
- 2 shrimp
- 2 shiitake mushrooms
- ½ cup cooked chicken, diced

Instructions:

1. **Make Egg Mixture:** Whisk eggs with dashi, soy sauce, and mirin.
2. **Fill Cups:** Place shrimp, mushrooms, and chicken in ramekins, pour in egg mixture.
3. **Steam:** Steam for 15 minutes until set.

Nikujaga (Japanese Meat and Potato Stew)

Ingredients:

- ½ lb thinly sliced beef
- 2 potatoes, diced
- 1 carrot, sliced
- 1 onion, sliced
- 1 cup dashi
- 2 tbsp soy sauce
- 1 tbsp mirin
- 1 tsp sugar

Instructions:

1. **Cook Beef & Onions:** Sauté in a pot.
2. **Add Vegetables & Simmer:** Pour in dashi, soy sauce, mirin, and sugar. Cook until potatoes are tender.
3. **Serve:** Enjoy warm with rice.

Sukiyaki (Japanese Hot Pot with Beef & Vegetables)

Ingredients:

- ½ lb thinly sliced beef
- 1 block tofu, cubed
- 1 cup napa cabbage, chopped
- ½ cup shiitake mushrooms
- 1 carrot, sliced
- 1 green onion, chopped
- 2 cups dashi
- 2 tbsp soy sauce
- 1 tbsp mirin
- 1 tbsp sugar

Instructions:

1. **Make Broth:** Heat dashi, soy sauce, mirin, and sugar in a pot.
2. **Add Ingredients:** Arrange beef, tofu, vegetables, and mushrooms in the broth.
3. **Cook & Serve:** Simmer and serve hot.

Shabu-Shabu (Japanese Hot Pot with Thinly Sliced Meat)

Ingredients:

- ½ lb thinly sliced beef or pork
- 1 block tofu, cubed
- 1 cup napa cabbage
- ½ cup shiitake mushrooms
- 2 cups dashi
- 1 tbsp soy sauce
- 1 tbsp mirin
- 1 tbsp sesame sauce (for dipping)

Instructions:

1. **Heat Broth:** Bring dashi, soy sauce, and mirin to a simmer.
2. **Dip & Swirl:** Cook meat and vegetables by briefly dipping in the hot broth.
3. **Serve:** Enjoy with sesame sauce or ponzu.

Nabe (Japanese Hot Pot with Various Ingredients)

Ingredients:

- ½ lb chicken or seafood
- 1 block tofu, cubed
- 1 cup napa cabbage
- ½ cup mushrooms
- 2 cups dashi
- 2 tbsp soy sauce
- 1 tbsp miso paste
- 1 green onion, chopped

Instructions:

1. **Heat Broth:** Mix dashi, soy sauce, and miso paste in a pot.
2. **Add Ingredients:** Arrange meat, tofu, vegetables, and mushrooms.
3. **Simmer & Serve:** Cook and enjoy straight from the pot.

Yosenabe (Mixed Japanese Hot Pot)

Ingredients:

- 4 cups dashi
- ½ lb thinly sliced chicken, pork, or seafood
- ½ block tofu, cubed
- 1 cup napa cabbage, chopped
- ½ cup mushrooms (shiitake or enoki)
- ½ cup daikon radish, sliced
- 1 carrot, sliced
- 1 tbsp soy sauce
- 1 tbsp mirin

Instructions:

1. **Prepare Broth:** Heat dashi, soy sauce, and mirin in a pot.
2. **Add Ingredients:** Arrange protein, tofu, vegetables, and mushrooms in the broth.
3. **Simmer & Serve:** Cook until all ingredients are tender, then serve hot.

Oden (Japanese Winter Hot Pot)

Ingredients:

- 4 cups dashi
- 1 tbsp soy sauce
- 1 tbsp mirin
- 1 tbsp sake
- 4 fish cakes (kamaboko, chikuwa, hanpen)
- 2 boiled eggs
- 4 daikon radish slices
- 4 tofu pouches (filled with mochi or vegetables)
- 4 konnyaku pieces

Instructions:

1. **Simmer Broth:** Heat dashi, soy sauce, mirin, and sake.
2. **Add Ingredients:** Simmer fish cakes, eggs, daikon, and tofu pouches for at least 30 minutes.
3. **Serve:** Enjoy warm with mustard or miso.

Hiyayakko (Chilled Tofu with Toppings)

Ingredients:

- 1 block silken tofu
- 1 green onion, chopped
- 1 tbsp soy sauce
- 1 tbsp grated ginger
- ½ tbsp bonito flakes (optional)

Instructions:

1. **Chill Tofu:** Cut tofu into cubes and refrigerate.
2. **Add Toppings:** Garnish with green onions, ginger, and bonito flakes.
3. **Serve:** Drizzle with soy sauce and enjoy.

Gyoza (Japanese Pan-Fried Dumplings)

Ingredients:

- ½ lb ground pork
- ½ cup cabbage, finely chopped
- 1 green onion, minced
- 1 clove garlic, minced
- 1 tsp grated ginger
- 1 tbsp soy sauce
- 1 tsp sesame oil
- 20 gyoza wrappers

Instructions:

1. **Make Filling:** Mix pork, cabbage, green onion, garlic, ginger, soy sauce, and sesame oil.
2. **Fill Wrappers:** Place filling in wrappers, seal edges with water.
3. **Cook:** Pan-fry in oil until crispy, then add water, cover, and steam for 5 minutes.

Karaage (Japanese Fried Chicken)

Ingredients:

- ½ lb boneless chicken thighs, cut into bite-sized pieces
- 2 tbsp soy sauce
- 1 tbsp sake
- 1 tsp grated ginger
- ½ cup potato starch
- Oil for frying

Instructions:

1. **Marinate Chicken:** Mix chicken with soy sauce, sake, and ginger. Let sit for 30 minutes.
2. **Coat & Fry:** Dredge in potato starch and deep-fry until golden brown.
3. **Serve:** Enjoy hot with lemon wedges.

Agedashi Tofu (Deep-Fried Tofu in Dashi Sauce)

Ingredients:

- 1 block firm tofu, cut into cubes
- ½ cup potato starch
- Oil for frying
- ½ cup dashi
- 1 tbsp soy sauce
- 1 tbsp mirin
- 1 green onion, chopped

Instructions:

1. **Prepare Tofu:** Pat dry, coat with potato starch, and deep-fry until golden.
2. **Make Sauce:** Heat dashi, soy sauce, and mirin.
3. **Serve:** Pour sauce over tofu and garnish with green onions.

Tamagoyaki (Japanese Rolled Omelet)

Ingredients:

- 3 eggs
- 1 tbsp sugar
- 1 tbsp soy sauce
- 1 tbsp mirin
- 1 tsp dashi (optional)
- Oil for frying

Instructions:

1. **Whisk Eggs:** Beat eggs with sugar, soy sauce, mirin, and dashi.
2. **Cook in Layers:** Pour a thin layer into a rectangular pan, roll, and repeat.
3. **Slice & Serve:** Cut into pieces and serve warm.

Zaru Soba (Cold Buckwheat Noodles with Dipping Sauce)

Ingredients:

- 8 oz soba noodles
- 1 cup dashi
- ¼ cup soy sauce
- ¼ cup mirin
- 1 tsp wasabi
- 1 green onion, chopped

Instructions:

1. **Cook Soba:** Boil and rinse under cold water.
2. **Make Dipping Sauce:** Mix dashi, soy sauce, and mirin.
3. **Serve:** Dip soba in sauce with wasabi and green onions.

Kitsune Udon (Udon with Sweet Fried Tofu)

Ingredients:

- 2 cups dashi
- 2 tbsp soy sauce
- 1 tbsp mirin
- 1 tsp sugar
- 1 fried tofu pouch (aburaage)
- 1 serving udon noodles
- Green onions for garnish

Instructions:

1. **Prepare Broth:** Simmer dashi, soy sauce, mirin, and sugar.
2. **Cook Udon:** Boil noodles and drain.
3. **Assemble:** Pour broth over noodles, top with tofu and green onions.

Nabeyaki Udon (Hot Pot Udon with Tempura & Egg)

Ingredients:

- 2 cups dashi
- 2 tbsp soy sauce
- 1 tbsp mirin
- 1 serving udon noodles
- 1 egg
- 2 shrimp tempura
- ½ cup mushrooms
- 1 green onion, chopped

Instructions:

1. **Prepare Broth:** Simmer dashi, soy sauce, and mirin.
2. **Cook Udon:** Boil and transfer to a clay pot.
3. **Add Toppings:** Crack an egg into the soup, add tempura and mushrooms, and simmer until egg is slightly set.

Somen (Chilled Thin Noodles with Dipping Sauce)

Ingredients:

- 8 oz somen noodles
- 2 cups ice water
- 1 cup tsuyu (noodle dipping sauce)
- 1 green onion, chopped
- 1 tsp grated ginger
- 1 tbsp sesame seeds

Instructions:

1. **Cook Somen:** Boil noodles for 2 minutes, rinse under cold water, and drain.
2. **Prepare Dipping Sauce:** Serve tsuyu chilled with green onions, ginger, and sesame seeds.
3. **Serve:** Dip noodles into sauce and enjoy.

Hiyashi Chuka (Cold Ramen Salad)

Ingredients:

- 8 oz cooked ramen noodles, chilled
- 1 cucumber, julienned
- 1 carrot, julienned
- ½ cup cooked chicken or ham, shredded
- 1 egg, cooked into a thin omelet and sliced
- ¼ cup soy sauce
- 2 tbsp rice vinegar
- 1 tbsp sugar
- 1 tbsp sesame oil

Instructions:

1. **Make Dressing:** Mix soy sauce, vinegar, sugar, and sesame oil.
2. **Assemble Salad:** Place noodles on a plate, top with cucumber, carrot, chicken, and egg.
3. **Serve:** Drizzle dressing over and enjoy cold.

Ochazuke (Rice with Green Tea Broth)

Ingredients:

- 1 cup cooked rice
- ½ cup green tea or dashi
- 1 tsp soy sauce
- 1 tbsp sesame seeds
- ½ sheet nori, crumbled
- 1 piece salted salmon or umeboshi (pickled plum)

Instructions:

1. **Assemble Rice Bowl:** Place rice in a bowl, top with salmon or umeboshi.
2. **Pour Broth:** Pour hot green tea or dashi over the rice.
3. **Serve:** Garnish with sesame seeds and nori.

Saba Shioyaki (Grilled Salted Mackerel)

Ingredients:

- 1 fillet mackerel (saba)
- 1 tsp sea salt
- 1 tbsp sake
- Lemon wedges for serving

Instructions:

1. **Prepare Fish:** Rinse fillet, pat dry, and rub with sake and salt.
2. **Grill:** Cook skin-side down over medium heat for 5 minutes per side.
3. **Serve:** Garnish with lemon wedges and serve with rice.

Tai Meshi (Sea Bream Rice)

Ingredients:

- 1 whole sea bream (tai), cleaned
- 2 cups rice
- 2 ½ cups dashi
- 2 tbsp soy sauce
- 1 tbsp mirin
- 1 tsp salt
- 1 green onion, chopped

Instructions:

1. **Prepare Fish:** Lightly salt the fish and grill until golden.
2. **Cook Rice:** Combine rice, dashi, soy sauce, mirin, and salt in a rice cooker.
3. **Steam Fish:** Place the grilled fish on top of the rice and cook together.
4. **Serve:** Flake the fish, mix into the rice, and garnish with green onions.

Buta no Shogayaki (Ginger Pork Stir-Fry)

Ingredients:

- ½ lb thinly sliced pork loin
- 1 tbsp soy sauce
- 1 tbsp sake
- 1 tbsp mirin
- 1 tsp sugar
- 1 tbsp grated ginger
- 1 tbsp vegetable oil

Instructions:

1. **Make Sauce:** Mix soy sauce, sake, mirin, sugar, and ginger.
2. **Stir-Fry Pork:** Heat oil in a pan, cook pork until golden.
3. **Add Sauce & Serve:** Pour in sauce, cook until coated, and serve with rice.

Katsu Curry (Pork Cutlet with Japanese Curry Sauce)

Ingredients:

- 1 pork cutlet (tonkatsu)
- 1 cup cooked rice
- 1 cup Japanese curry sauce (store-bought or homemade)
- ½ onion, chopped
- 1 carrot, chopped
- 1 potato, diced

Instructions:

1. **Make Curry Sauce:** Sauté onion, carrot, and potato, then simmer with curry mix and water.
2. **Cook Tonkatsu:** Fry breaded pork cutlet until crispy, then slice.
3. **Serve:** Place tonkatsu over rice and pour curry sauce on top.

Hayashi Rice (Japanese Beef Stew with Demi-Glace Sauce)

Ingredients:

- ½ lb thinly sliced beef
- ½ onion, sliced
- 1 cup mushrooms, sliced
- 2 tbsp butter
- 2 tbsp flour
- 1 cup beef broth
- ½ cup tomato puree
- 1 tbsp Worcestershire sauce
- 1 tsp sugar
- 1 cup cooked rice

Instructions:

1. **Sauté Ingredients:** Cook beef, onions, and mushrooms in butter.
2. **Make Sauce:** Stir in flour, then add broth, tomato puree, Worcestershire sauce, and sugar. Simmer until thick.
3. **Serve:** Spoon over rice and enjoy.

Omurice (Omelet Rice with Ketchup Sauce)

Ingredients:

- 1 cup cooked rice
- ½ onion, chopped
- ½ cup chicken, diced
- 2 tbsp ketchup
- 1 tbsp soy sauce
- 2 eggs
- 1 tbsp milk
- 1 tbsp butter

Instructions:

1. **Make Fried Rice:** Sauté onions and chicken, then add rice, ketchup, and soy sauce.
2. **Cook Omelet:** Beat eggs with milk, cook into a thin omelet in butter.
3. **Assemble:** Place fried rice on one side of the omelet, fold over, and serve.

Hambagu (Japanese Hamburger Steak)

Ingredients:

- ½ lb ground beef
- ½ small onion, finely chopped
- ¼ cup panko breadcrumbs
- 1 egg
- 1 tbsp milk
- 1 tbsp Worcestershire sauce
- 1 tbsp ketchup
- 1 tbsp soy sauce

Instructions:

1. **Make Patty:** Mix beef, onion, panko, egg, milk, salt, and pepper. Shape into patties.
2. **Cook:** Sear patties in a pan until browned on both sides.
3. **Make Sauce:** Mix Worcestershire sauce, ketchup, and soy sauce. Pour over patties and simmer.
4. **Serve:** Enjoy with rice or vegetables.

Japanese Potato Salad (Creamy Japanese-Style Potato Salad)

Ingredients:

- 2 large potatoes, peeled and diced
- ½ cup cucumber, thinly sliced
- ½ cup carrot, thinly sliced
- ¼ cup corn (optional)
- ¼ cup ham, chopped (optional)
- 2 tbsp Japanese mayonnaise (Kewpie)
- 1 tsp rice vinegar
- ½ tsp sugar
- Salt and pepper to taste

Instructions:

1. **Boil Potatoes & Vegetables:** Cook potatoes until tender. Lightly blanch carrots.
2. **Mash & Mix:** Lightly mash potatoes, leaving some chunks. Mix with cucumber, carrot, corn, and ham.
3. **Season & Serve:** Stir in mayo, vinegar, sugar, salt, and pepper. Chill before serving.

Kinpira Gobo (Stir-Fried Burdock Root & Carrot)

Ingredients:

- 1 burdock root (gobo), julienned
- 1 small carrot, julienned
- 1 tbsp soy sauce
- 1 tbsp mirin
- 1 tsp sugar
- 1 tsp sesame oil
- 1 tsp sesame seeds

Instructions:

1. **Prepare Burdock:** Soak burdock root in water for 10 minutes to remove bitterness.
2. **Stir-Fry:** Heat sesame oil, cook burdock and carrot until slightly softened.
3. **Season & Serve:** Add soy sauce, mirin, and sugar, stir until glazed. Sprinkle sesame seeds before serving.

Tsukemono (Japanese Pickles)

Ingredients:

- 1 cucumber, thinly sliced
- ½ tsp salt
- 1 tbsp rice vinegar
- 1 tsp sugar
- ½ tsp soy sauce

Instructions:

1. **Salt the Cucumber:** Massage cucumber slices with salt and let sit for 10 minutes.
2. **Rinse & Marinate:** Rinse, then mix with vinegar, sugar, and soy sauce.
3. **Serve:** Let sit for at least 30 minutes before serving.

Daifuku (Mochi Filled with Sweet Red Bean Paste)

Ingredients:

- 1 cup glutinous rice flour (shiratamako)
- ½ cup water
- ¼ cup sugar
- ½ cup sweet red bean paste (anko)
- Cornstarch for dusting

Instructions:

1. **Make Mochi Dough:** Mix flour, water, and sugar. Microwave for 2 minutes, stir, then microwave for another minute.
2. **Shape:** Dust hands with cornstarch, take a small piece of mochi, and wrap around red bean paste.
3. **Serve:** Shape into smooth balls and enjoy.

Dorayaki (Japanese Pancakes with Red Bean Filling)

Ingredients:

- 1 cup flour
- 2 eggs
- ¼ cup sugar
- 1 tbsp honey
- ½ tsp baking powder
- ½ cup water
- ½ cup sweet red bean paste (anko)

Instructions:

1. **Make Batter:** Whisk eggs, sugar, honey, and baking powder. Add flour and water to make a smooth batter.
2. **Cook Pancakes:** Pour small rounds of batter onto a pan and cook until golden brown.
3. **Assemble:** Spread red bean paste on one pancake and top with another.

Matcha Warabi Mochi (Chewy Matcha Starch Dessert)

Ingredients:

- ½ cup warabi starch (or cornstarch)
- 1 cup water
- 3 tbsp sugar
- 1 tbsp matcha powder
- Kinako (roasted soybean flour) for dusting

Instructions:

1. **Cook Mochi:** Mix starch, water, sugar, and matcha. Heat while stirring until thick.
2. **Chill & Cut:** Pour onto a tray, cool, then cut into cubes.
3. **Serve:** Dust with kinako and enjoy.

Mitarashi Dango (Grilled Rice Dumplings with Sweet Soy Sauce)

Ingredients:

- 1 cup glutinous rice flour (shiratamako)
- ½ cup water
- 2 tbsp soy sauce
- 2 tbsp sugar
- 1 tbsp mirin
- 1 tsp cornstarch

Instructions:

1. **Make Dango:** Mix rice flour and water to form a dough. Shape into balls and boil until they float.
2. **Grill:** Skewer the dumplings and grill until slightly charred.
3. **Make Sauce & Serve:** Simmer soy sauce, sugar, mirin, and cornstarch until thick. Brush over dango and serve.

Anmitsu (Japanese Dessert with Agar Jelly, Fruits & Sweet Syrup)

Ingredients:

- 1 cup kanten (agar) jelly, cubed
- ½ cup sweet red bean paste (anko)
- ½ cup fresh fruits (strawberries, kiwi, oranges)
- 1 tbsp kuromitsu (black sugar syrup)

Instructions:

1. **Prepare Kanten Jelly:** Dissolve kanten powder in hot water, pour into a mold, and chill until set.
2. **Assemble Dessert:** Place jelly cubes, fruits, and anko in a bowl.
3. **Serve:** Drizzle with kuromitsu syrup before eating.

Taiyaki (Fish-Shaped Pastry Filled with Red Bean Paste)

Ingredients:

- 1 cup flour
- ½ tsp baking powder
- 1 egg
- 1 tbsp sugar
- ½ cup milk
- ½ cup sweet red bean paste (anko)

Instructions:

1. **Make Batter:** Whisk flour, baking powder, egg, sugar, and milk.
2. **Cook in Taiyaki Mold:** Pour batter into a heated fish-shaped taiyaki mold, add anko, then cover with more batter.
3. **Serve:** Cook until golden brown and enjoy warm.

www.ingramcontent.com/pod-product-compliance
Lightning Source LLC
LaVergne TN
LVHW061956070526
838199LV00060B/4160